D1036881

CHARLIE AND THE
GREAT GLASS ELEVATOR: A PLAY

Just imagine what it must be like to take off with Willy
Wonka and Charlie Bucket in the amazing Great Glass
Elevator! Now you, too, can zoom into orbit, brave the
Vermicious Knids and meet the President of the U.S.A.
in this excellent dramatization of Roald Dahl's best-
selling adventure.

The book contains the full script, staging instructions
and lighting suggestions, as well as some helpful hints for
making scenery and props. Tried and tested in schools,
Charlie and the Great Glass Elevator: A Play is simple to
stage and will provide hours of enjoyment for any bunch
of enthusiastic actors, whether at home or in school.

Roald Dahl's *Charlie and the Chocolate Factory* and *James
and the Giant Peach* have both been adapted for the stage
by Richard George.

ROALD DAHL'S

CHARLIE AND THE GREAT GLASS ELEVATOR: A PLAY

Adapted by Richard R. George

Introduction by Roald Dahl

London
GEORGE ALLEN & UNWIN
Boston   Sydney

George Allen & Unwin (Publishers) Ltd
40 Museum Street, London WC1A 1LU, UK

George Allen & Unwin (Publishers) Ltd
Park Lane, Hemel Hempstead, Herts HP2 4TE, UK

Allen & Unwin Inc.,
Fifty Cross Street, Winchester, Mass 01890, USA

George Allen & Unwin Australia Pty Ltd,
8 Napier Street, North Sydney, NSW 2060, Australia

First published in 1984

British Library Cataloguing in Publication Data

George, Richard R.
    Charlie and the great glass elevator.
    I. Title   II. Dahl, Roald. Charlie and
    the great glass elevator
    812'.54   PR6507.E/

ISBN 0-04-792014-9

Made and printed in Great Britain by
Richard Clay (The Chaucer Press) Ltd, Bungay, Suffolk
Filmset in Monophoto Baskerville by
Northumberland Press Ltd, Gateshead

For my wife, Susan …
who loves me
and supports me,
in spite of
the crazy hours
I choose to write!

CONTENTS

INTRODUCTION

That clever American schoolteacher, Richard George, who made *Charlie and the Chocolate Factory* into a play, has now done the same thing with *Charlie and the Great Glass Elevator*. This is a more simplified version of the original than the first one was, and for that reason I think it will be even easier to stage. School plays are hard enough to put on at the best of times, and the over-worked teachers who have to produce and direct them will certainly appreciate this simplicity.

ROALD DAHL

CHARLIE AND THE
GREAT GLASS ELEVATOR

CAST OF CHARACTERS
(In order of appearance)

Narrator
Grandma Josephine
Mr Wonka
Grandma Georgina
Charlie
Grandpa Joe
Grandpa George
Shuckworth
Showler
Shanks
Ground Control
President
Mr Bucket
Mrs Bucket
Chief of Staff
Miss Tibbs
Premier Yugetoff
Assistant Premier Chu-on-Dat
Chief Financial Adviser
Chief Interpreter
Walter Wall

SCENE 1

NARRATOR *enters in front of curtain.*

NARRATOR: Hi everybody! Charlie is back! Starting where *Charlie and the Chocolate Factory* left off – in the Great Glass Elevator – this story takes Charlie, Mr Willy Wonka, and Charlie's parents and grandparents on a most extraordinary series of adventures. Now the last time we saw Charlie, he was riding high above his home town in the Great Glass Elevator. Only a short while before, Mr Wonka had told him that the whole gigantic fabulous Chocolate Factory was his, and now our small friend is returning in triumph with his entire family to take over ... or at least so he thinks. Well ... uh ... we won't go into that now. Oh look! There's the Great Glass Elevator now! It's just coming into view! See it? Here it comes! [*Pointing towards centre stage*]

    [*Curtain opens and reveals Great Glass Elevator with* CHARLIE, MR WONKA *and* CHARLIE'S FAMILY *all inside and frozen in place:* CHARLIE *and* MR WONKA *are standing near a control panel;* GRANDPA JOE *and* MR *and* MRS BUCKET *are standing near the bed;* GRANDMA JOSEPHINE,

GRANDMA GEORGINA *and* GRANDPA GEORGE *are in bed*]

Since the Great Glass Elevator is presently in mid-air I cannot myself travel right up next to them, but I will introduce them to you from here. The three very old people in the bed are Grandma Josephine, Grandma Georgina, and Grandpa George. As you remember, Grandpa Joe had got out of bed to go around the Chocolate Factory with Charlie, so he is standing next to Charlie's other grandparents. The other two standing next to Grandpa Joe are Mr and Mrs Bucket, otherwise known as Charlie's parents. Now Mr Wonka is very easy to point out because he is the super-incredible, wonderfully handsome elderly gentleman known as the world's most famous chocolate-maker extraordinary, stand-ing next to the control panel. And last of all, but cer-tainly not least is our hero ... Charlie Bucket. He is a delightful boy. He's the one standing next to Mr Wonka by the control panel. Mr Wonka truly loves this boy. Why, he'd have to if he is giving him his entire Chocolate Factory! Yes, Charlie is just like a son to Mr Wonka. [*Looking wistfully off to the side*] Yes ... well ... uh ... I think it's time we got back to our story. The Great Glass Elevator is presently a thousand feet up and cruising nicely. The sky is a brilliant blue. Everybody on board is wildly excited at the thought of going to live in the famous

Chocolate Factory. Grandpa Joe is singing. Charlie ... well ... he is simply jumping up and down. And look at Mr and Mrs Bucket. They're smiling for the first time in years, and the three old ones in the bed are grinning at one another with their pink toothless gums. You know, perhaps if we are quiet ... I mean very quiet ... maybe we can hear what is happening on the Great Glass Elevator right now. Shhh ... Yes ... I can hear them now.

[NARRATOR *exits. All come to life*]

GRANDMA JOSEPHINE: What in the world keeps this thing up in the air?

MR WONKA: Skyhooks.

GRANDMA JOSEPHINE: You amaze me!

MR WONKA: Dear lady, you are new to the scene. When you have been with us a little longer, nothing will amaze you.

GRANDMA JOSEPHINE: These skyhooks ... I assume one end is hooked on to this contraption we're riding in. Right?

MR WONKA [*Matter-of-factly*]: Right.

GRANDMA JOSEPHINE: What's the other end hooked on to?

MR WONKA [*Ignoring the question*]: Every day I get deafer and deafer. Remind me, please, to call up my doctor the moment we get back.

GRANDMA JOSEPHINE: Charlie, I don't think I trust this gentleman very much.

GRANDMA GEORGINA: Nor do I. He footles around.

CHARLIE [*Leaning over and whispering to the two old women*]: Please, don't spoil everything. Mr Wonka is a fantastic man. He's my friend. I love him.

GRANDPA JOE [*Whispering*]: Charlie's right. Now you be quiet, Josie, and don't make trouble.

MR WONKA [*Excitedly*]: We must hurry! We have so much time and so little to do! No! Wait! Strike that! Reverse it! Thank you! Now back to the factory! [*Clapping his hands once and springing two feet in the air with two feet*] Back we fly to the factory! But we must go *up* before we can come down! We must go *higher* and *higher*!

GRANDMA JOSEPHINE: What did I tell you! The man's cracked!

GRANDPA JOE: Be quiet Josie, Mr Wonka knows exactly what he's doing.

GRANDMA GEORGINA: He's cracked as a crab!

MR WONKA [*Yelling*]: We must go higher! We must go tremendously high! Hold onto your stomachs!
[*He presses a brown button; the Elevator shakes and makes a whooshing noise as if accelerating. Everybody clutches hold of everybody else and the rushing, whooshing sound of the wind outside grows louder and louder*]

GRANDMA JOSEPHINE [*Yelling*]: Stop! Joe, you make him stop! I want to get off!

GRANDMA GEORGINA [*Yelling*]: Save us!

GRANDPA GEORGE [*Yelling*]: Go down!

MR WONKA [*Yelling*]: No, no! We've got to go up!

ALL [*Except* MR WONKA, *shouting*]: Why up and not down?

MR WONKA [*Shouting*]: Because the higher we are when we start coming down, the faster we'll be going when we hit. We've got to be going at an absolutely sizzling speed when we hit!

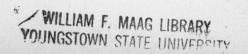

ALL [*Except* MR WONKA]: When we hit *what*?

MR WONKA: The factory of course!

GRANDMA JOSEPHINE: We'll all be pulpified!

GRANDMA GEORGINA: We'll be scrambled like eggs!

MR WONKA: That is a chance we shall have to take.

GRANDMA JOSEPHINE: You're joking! Tell us you're joking!

MR WONKA: Madam, I never joke.

GRANDMA GEORGINA: Oh, my dears! We'll all be lixivated, every one of us!

MR WONKA: More than likely.
> [GRANDMA JOSEPHINE *screams and disappears under the bedclothes.* GRANDMA GEORGINA *clutches* GRANDPA GEORGE *so tight that he looks as if he is changing shape.* MR *and* MRS BUCKET *stand hugging each other, speechless with fright. Only* CHARLIE *and* GRANDPA JOE *keep moderately cool*]

CHARLIE [*Beginning to act just a little unsure of things*]: Mr Wonka! [*Yelling above the noise*] What I don't understand is why we've got to come down at such a terrific speed!

MR WONKA: My dear boy, if we don't come down at a terrific speed, we'll never burst our way back through the roof of the factory. It's not easy to punch a hole in a roof as strong as that.

CHARLIE: But there's a hole in it already. [*Still yelling*] We made it when we came out!

MR WONKA: Then we shall make another! Two holes are better than one. Any mouse will tell you that.
[*Characters go to frozen-action position.* NARRATOR *enters in front of curtain off to the side: spotlight*]

NARRATOR: Higher and higher rushed the Great Glass Elevator until soon they could see the countries and oceans of the earth spread out below them like a map. It was all very beautiful, but when you are standing on a glass floor looking down, it gives you a nasty feeling. You know, I believe even Charlie is beginning to feel frightened now. Look at the look on his face and notice how tightly he is gripping Grandpa Joe's hand.

[NARRATOR *goes to frozen-action position: spotlight off. Characters move out of frozen action*]

CHARLIE: I'm scared, Grandpa.

GRANDPA JOE [*Putting an arm round* CHARLIE'S *shoulders and holding him close*]: So am I, Charlie ... so am I.

CHARLIE: Mr Wonka! [*Shouting*] Don't you think this is about high enough?

MR WONKA: Very nearly, but not quite. Don't talk to me now, please. Don't disturb me. I must watch things very carefully at this stage. Split-second timing, my boy, that's what it's got to be. You see this green button. I must press it at exactly the right instant. If I'm just half a second late, then we'll go ... too high!

GRANDPA JOE: What happens if we go too high?

MR WONKA: Do please stop talking and let me concentrate!

[NARRATOR *comes out of frozen-action: spotlight on*]

NARRATOR: Now at this precise moment, Grandma

Josephine, you might observe, is poking her head
out from under the sheets, peering over the edge
of the bed, and looking through the glass floor. As
you could well imagine, the sight that she beholds
is a frightening one. She sees the entire continent
of North America nearly two hundred miles below
and looking no bigger than a piece of candy. I'm
afraid that this is just too much for the old gal to
handle. She's very unpredictable! I fear that she
just might ...

[*Spotlight off* NARRATOR]

GRANDMA JOSEPHINE [*Interrupting with a scream*]:
Someone's got to stop this maniac!

[*She reaches out and grabs* MR WONKA *by the coat-
tails and yanks him backwards onto the bed*]

MR WONKA: No, no! Let me go! [*Frantically and strug-
gling to free himself*] I have things to see to! Don't
disturb the pilot!

GRANDMA JOSEPHINE [*Shrieking and shaking* MR
WONKA *wildly*]: You madman! You get us back
home this instant!

MR WONKA [*With a demanding plea*]: Let me go! I've
got to press that button or we'll go too high! Let
me go! Let me go! [*Finally, in frustration, he signals*

frantically to CHARLIE] Charlie! [*Shouting*] Press the button! The green one! Quick! Quick! Quick! [CHARLIE *leaps across the Elevator and bangs his thumb down on the green button. As he does so, the sound of the Elevator totally stops and there is an eerie silence*] Too late! Oh, my goodness me, we're cooked! [*As* MR WONKA *says this, the bed is tilted up in the air at one end by means of a rope or wire and everyone behaves in a bouncy, floating fashion*] Now look what you've done!
  [*All action moving very slowly; it would be quite effective if a strobe light were used during all 'weightless' times*]

GRANDMA JOSEPHINE: What happened?

CHARLIE: Did we go too far?

MR WONKA: Too far? I'll say we went too far! You know where we've gone, my friends? We've gone into ORBIT! [*Everyone looks too flabbergasted to speak*] We are now rushing around the earth at seventeen thousand miles an hour. How does that grab you?

GRANDMA GEORGINA: I'm choking! [*Gasping*] I can't breathe!

MR WONKA: Of course you can't! There's no air up

here. [*He sort of swims across the Elevator to a button marked* OXYGEN *and presses it*] You'll be all right now ... breathe away.

CHARLIE: This is the queerest feeling. [*Swimming about*] I feel like a bubble.

GRANDPA JOE: It's great! It feels as though I don't weigh anything at all.

MR WONKA: You don't! None of us weighs anything ... not even one ounce.

GRANDMA GEORGINA: What piffle! I weigh eighty-seven pounds exactly.

MR WONKA: Not now you don't. You are completely weightless.

GRANDPA JOE: We've got you out of bed at last!

GRANDMA JOSEPHINE: Shut up and help us back!
    [GRANDPA GEORGE, GRANDMA GEORGINA
    and GRANDMA JOSEPHINE *are trying frantically
    to get back into bed*]

MR WONKA: Forget it! You'll never stay down. Just keep floating around and be happy.

GRANDMA GEORGINA: The man's a madman! Watch out, I say, or he'll lixivate the lot of us!
[*Curtain*]

End of Scene 1

SCENE 2

NARRATOR *enters in front of curtain, off to the side as usual: spotlight.*

NARRATOR: While the Great Glass Elevator and everybody inside is sort of ... uh ... should I say ... 'up in the air', there are other fantastic things happening. Why, did you know that just two days ago the United States of America successfully launched its first *Space Hotel*? That's right! It's kind of a gigantic sausage-shaped capsule no less than one thousand feet long. It's called Space Hotel U.S.A. and it's the marvel of the space age. [*Holding up a newspaper and reading from it*] It's in *all* the papers. It says here that it's got inside it a tennis court, a swimming pool, a gymnasium, a children's playroom and five hundred luxury bedrooms, each with a private bath. It says it's fully air-conditioned. My goodness ... it's even equipped with a gravity-making machine so that you don't even float about inside it. You can walk normally. It says here at the bottom that the Space Hotel U.S.A. is right now speeding round and round the earth at a height of two hundred and forty miles. Guests are supposed to be taken up and down by a taxi service of commuter capsules blasting off from Cape Kennedy every hour on the hour, Monday to Friday. But as yet there's nobody on board at all, not even an astronaut. [*Putting the newspaper down*] I guess the reason for this is that no one really believed such an enormous thing would ever get off the ground without blowing up. Well, it just goes to show you . . . things are not always as they seem. The launching has been a great success and now that the Space Hotel is safely in orbit, there's a tremendous hustle and bustle to send up the first guests. [*Looking around and acting secretively*] Now don't tell anybody, but I even heard a rumour that the President of the United States himself is going to be among the first to stay in the hotel. Oh well . . . who knows . . . but now listen . . . you can't send guests to a hotel unless there are lots of people there to look after them, and that explains why there is yet *another* interesting object orbiting the earth at this moment. That's right, I said another! Yes, it's a large Commuter Capsule containing the entire staff for Space Hotel U.S.A. I guess it's got managers, assistant managers, desk clerks, waitresses, bellhops, chambermaids, pastry chefs and hall porters. You'll never believe it but the capsule itself is manned by those phenomenally famous astronauts, Shuckworth, Shanks and Showler, all of whom are incredibly handsome,

clever and brave! Why ... there they come now ...
duck your heads everybody!

>[*Scene now shifts to opposite side of stage where
>action takes place with the three* ASTRONAUTS.
>NARRATOR *exits*]

SHUCKWORTH: Attention all passengers, friends,
relatives and countrymen ... this is your Captain
speaking! In exactly one hour, that's right, you
heard it, in exactly one hour ... we shall link up with
the Space Hotel U.S.A., your happy home for the
next ten years. [*Aside*] (Did I say ten years?) And
any moment now, if you look straight ahead, you
could catch your first glimpse of this magnificent
spaceship. Ah-ha! I see something there! [*Looking
forward with a hand over his eyes as in a salute*] That must
be it, folks! There's definitely something up there
ahead of us!

SHOWLER: Hey, that isn't our Space Hotel.

SHANKS: Holy rats! What in the name of Nebuchad-
nezzar is it?

SHUCKWORTH: Quick! Give me the telescope!
[*With one hand looking through the telescope and the other
grabbing a hand microphone*] Hello, Houston! There's
something crazy going on up here. There's a thing

orbiting ahead of us and it's not like any spaceship I've ever seen, that's for sure!

[*Ground Control can now be spotlit in front of the stage but off to the same side as the Commuter Capsule. Another spotlight on* ASTRONAUTS]

GROUND CONTROL: Describe it at once!

SHUCKWORTH: It's ... it's ... it's all made of glass and it's kind of square and it's got lots of people inside it! They're all floating about like fish in a tank!

GROUND CONTROL: How many astronauts on board?

SHUCKWORTH: They can't possibly be astronauts.

GROUND CONTROL: What makes you say that?

SHUCKWORTH: Because at least three of them are in nightshirts!

GROUND CONTROL: Don't be a fool, Shuckworth! Pull yourself together, man! This is serious!

SHUCKWORTH: I swear it! There's three of them in nightshirts! Two old women and one old man! I can see them clearly! I can even see their faces! Jeepers, they're older than Moses! They're about ninety years old!

[*He passes the telescope to the other two*]

GROUND CONTROL [*Shouting*]: You've gone mad, Shuckworth! You're fired! Give me Shanks!

SHANKS: Shanks speaking. Now listen here, Houston. There's these three old birds in nightshirts floating around in this crazy glass box and there's a funny little guy with a pointed beard wearing a black top hat and a plum-coloured velvet tail-coat and bottle-green trousers . . .

GROUND CONTROL [*Screaming*]: STOP!

SHANKS: Hold the phone! There's also a little boy about ten years old.

GROUND CONTROL [*Shouting*]: That's no boy, you idiot! That's an astronaut in disguise! It's a midget astronaut dressed up as a little boy! Those old people are astronauts too! They're all in disguise!

SHANKS: But who *are* they?

GROUND CONTROL: How in the world should I know? Are they heading for our Space Hotel?

SHANKS: That's exactly where they are heading. I can see the Space Hotel now about a mile ahead.

GROUND CONTROL [*Yelling*]: They're going to blow it up! This is desperate! This is ...
> [*Suddenly the voice is cut off and* SHANKS *hears a different voice. Enter* PRESIDENT'S *voice over the loudspeaker, but not seen*]

PRESIDENT: I'll take charge of this. Are you there, Shanks?

SHANKS: Of course I'm here. But how dare you butt in! Keep your big nose out of this! Who are you anyway?

PRESIDENT: This is the President of the United States.

SHANKS [*Sarcastically*]: And this is the Wizard of Oz. Who are you kidding?

PRESIDENT [*Angrily*]: Cut the piffle, Shanks! This is a national emergency!

SHANKS: Good grief! [*Turning to* SHUCKWORTH *and* SHOWLER] It really is the President. It's President Gillifrass himself! Well, *hello there*, Mr President, sir. How are *you* today?

PRESIDENT: How many people are there in that glass capsule?

SHANKS: Eight. All floating.

PRESIDENT: *Floating?*

SHANKS: We're outside the pull of gravity up here, Mr President. Everything floats. We'd be floating ourselves if we weren't strapped down. Didn't you know that?

PRESIDENT: Of course I knew it. What else can you tell me about that glass capsule?

SHANKS: There's a bed in it. A big double bed, and that's floating too.

PRESIDENT [*Seemingly upset*]: A bed? Whoever heard of a bed in a spacecraft!

SHANKS: It's a bed, I tell you!

PRESIDENT: You must be loopy, Shanks! You're dotty as a doughnut! [*In demanding fashion*] Let me talk to Showler!

SHOWLER: Showler here, Mr President. [*Taking the*

mike from SHANKS] It is a great honour to talk to you, Mr President, sir.

PRESIDENT: Oh, shut up! Just tell me what you see.

SHOWLER: It's a bed all right, Mr President. I can see it through my telescope. It's got sheets and blankets and a mattress ...

PRESIDENT [*Interrupting in a yell*]: That's not a bed, you drivelling thickwit! Can't you understand it's a trick! It's a bomb! It's a bomb disguised as a bed! They're going to blow up our magnificent Space Hotel!

SHOWLER: Who's *they*, Mr President, sir?

PRESIDENT [*Thinking*]: I've just thought of something. Don't you have a television camera up there on the front of your spacecraft, Showler?

SHOWLER: Sure do, Mr President.

PRESIDENT: Then switch it on, you nit, and let all of us down here get a look at this object!

SHOWLER: I never thought of that. No *wonder* you're the President. Here goes!

[*He reaches over to turn on the switch: spotlight on* NARRATOR *on other side of the stage; spotlight off* ASTRONAUTS *and Ground Control*]

NARRATOR: What a moment! What fear! What apprehension! Just imagine ... over five hundred million people all over the world who have been listening in on their radios, have rushed to their television sets. What an electrifying experience! [*Curtain opens with no stage lighting at first, but as the* NARRATOR *continues the lighting brightens a bit*] Everyone's waiting! The whole world! There! It's starting to show up. We're starting to see exactly what Shuckworth and Shanks and Showler were seeing ... a weird glass box in splendid orbit around the earth. And inside the box, seen not too clearly but seen nonetheless, are seven grown-ups and one small boy and a big double bed, all floating. Three of the grown-ups are bare-legged and wearing nightshirts. These astronauts – [*Aside*] or at least that's what everyone is calling them – appear to be so tough and strong they don't even bother to wear space-suits. Everyone is wondering who they are. All across America and Canada and Russia and England and Japan and India and China and Africa and France and Germany and everywhere else in the world a kind of panic is beginning to take hold of the television-watchers. Who are they? What

is it they have? What are they going to do?
  [*Spotlight is now turned off* ASTRONAUTS *and
  stage lights brought up*]

PRESIDENT [*Interrupting in an anxious voice*]: Keep well
  clear of them, Showler! I don't trust them! Wait for
  further orders before you do anything. Do you
  understand, Showler?

SHOWLER: Yes sir, Mr President, sir! I sure will! I'll
  do just as you say! This is strange! This is scary!
  [*Spotlight is now turned off* ASTRONAUTS *and
  stage lights brought up*]

End of Scene 2

SCENE 3

MR WONKA: It's a good thing someone bumped into that radio button a little while ago. Turn off the radio, Charlie. [CHARLIE *pushes a button in the Elevator wall*] What a load of luck! We've landed ourselves in the middle of the biggest space operation of all time!

GRANDMA JOSEPHINE: We've landed ourselves in the middle of a nasty mess, if you ask me! Turn back at once!

CHARLIE: *No*, Grandma! We've *got* to watch it now! We *must* see the Commuter Capsule linking up with the Space Hotel!
> [MR WONKA *floats up to Charlie, puts his arm around him and whispers to him as an aside*]

MR WONKA: Let's beat them to it, Charlie. Let's get there first and go aboard the Space Hotel ourselves!

CHARLIE [*Gaping and gulping*]: It's impossible. You've got to have all sorts of special gadgets to link up with another spacecraft, Mr Wonka.

MR WONKA: My Elevator could link up with a croco-
dile if it had to. Just leave it to me, my boy!

CHARLIE: Grandpa Joe! Did you hear that? We're
going to link up with the Space Hotel and go on
board!

GRANDPA JOE [*Shouting*]: *Yippeeeee*! What a brilliant
thought, sir! What a staggering idea!
[*He grabs* MR WONKA'S *hand and shakes it like a
thermometer*]

GRANDMA JOSEPHINE: Be quiet, you barmy old bat!
We're in a hot enough stew already! I want to go
home!

GRANDMA GEORGINA: Me, too!

MR BUCKET: What if they come after us?

MRS BUCKET: What if they capture us?

GRANDPA GEORGE: What if they shoot us?

MR WONKA: What if my beard were made of green
spinach? Bunkum and tummyrot! You'll never get
anywhere if you go about what-iffing like that. We
want no what-iffers around here, right Charlie? Off

we go, then! Grandpa Joe, sir, kindly station yourself beside that silver button there ... yes, that's the one. And you, Charlie, go over and stay floating beside that little golden button near the ceiling. I must tell you that each of these buttons fires booster rockets from different places outside the Elevator. That's how we change direction. Grandpa Joe's rockets turn us to starboard, to the right. Charlie's turn us to port, to the left. Mine make us go higher or lower or faster or slower. All ready?

CHARLIE: No! Wait! How do I get over there? [*Pointing with his finger to the other side of the Elevator*] I can't seem to get anywhere. What do I do?

    [*He thrashes his arms and legs violently, like a drowning swimmer, but goes nowhere*]

MR WONKA: My dear boy, you can't *swim* in this stuff. It isn't water you know. It's air, and very thin air at that. You have to use jet propulsion. Watch me. First, you take a deep breath, then you make a small round hole with your mouth and you simply blow as hard as you can. If you blow downward, you jet propel yourself up. If you blow to the left, you shoot off to the right, and so on. You manoeuvre yourself like a spacecraft, but using your mouth as a booster rocket.

    [*Suddenly everyone begins practising the art of flying*

about, with GRANDMA GEORGINA *particularly
causing the most bedlam by crashing into everyone*]

GRANDMA GEORGINA [*Yelling thoughtlessly*]: Out of
my way! Out of my way!
[*Add spotlight on* ASTRONAUTS *and then dim stage
lights*]

PRESIDENT [*Shouting*]: What in the world are they
doing?

SHOWLER: Looks like some kind of war-dance, Mr
President.

PRESIDENT: You mean they're Indians!

SHOWLER: I didn't say that, sir.

PRESIDENT: Oh, yes you did, Showler.

SHOWLER: Oh, no I didn't, Mr President.

PRESIDENT [*Yelling*]: SILENCE! You're muddling
me up.
[*Spotlight on* ASTRONAUTS *is now turned off.
Stage brightens and action resumes in Elevator*]

MR WONKA: *PLEASE! PLEASE! Do* stop flying about!

Keep still everybody, so we can get on with the docking!

GRANDMA GEORGINA: You miserable old mackerel! [*Disgustedly*] Just when we start having a bit of fun, you want to stop it!

    [*Everyone settles down immediately*]

MR WONKA: All set, Charlie and Grandpa Joe, sir?

CHARLIE: All set, Mr Wonka.

MR WONKA: I'll give the orders! I'm the pilot. Don't fire your rockets until I tell you. Here we go ... steady as you go! Starboard ten degrees! ... Steady! Steady! Keep her there ... Good ... We're hovering directly underneath the tail of the Space Hotel. [*Pointing ahead*] There's the docking entrance. It won't be long now. Port a fraction ... Steady! ... Starboard a bit! Good ... Good ... Easy does it ... We're nearly there ...

    [*Curtain*]

End of Scene 3

SCENE 4

NARRATOR *enters in front of curtain off to the side as usual: spotlight.*

NARRATOR: Wow! Well if you think there is a lot of excitement on the Great Glass Elevator, you're right! But what you don't know is that there is also a great deal happening right now at the White House! Now we already know that millions of people around the world, having seen on television what is going on, are sitting frightfully on the edge of their seats. Just as they are fearful of what might soon happen, so too is the President of the United States of America, Lancelot R. Gilligrass, the most powerful man on earth. In this moment of crisis, he has summoned all his most powerful advisers urgently into his presence. The President's Military Chief of Staff, his Chief Financial Adviser, his cat, the famous Mrs Taubsypuss, and the Vice-President, a huge lady of eighty-nine by the name of Miss Tibbs, are all there. Now Miss Tibbs is the power behind the throne. She has been the President's nurse since he was a baby and some people say that she is as strict with the President now as when he was a little boy. She takes no nonsense from anyone and is the terror of the White House, and even the Head of the F.B.I. breaks into a sweat when summoned into her presence. Only the President is allowed to call her 'Nanny'. But now, this very moment, all eyes in the Presidential study are riveted to the TV screen as the small glass object slides smoothly up behind the giant Space Hotel.

[*Spotlight off* NARRATOR; *spotlight on Presidential Study area (formerly Ground Control).* PRESIDENT *is seen for the first time*]

PRESIDENT [*Shouting*]: They're going to link up! They're going on board our Space Hotel!

CHIEF OF STAFF [*Screaming*]: They're going to blow it up! Let's blow *them* up first – crash bang wallop bang-bang-bang-bang-bang. [*As he yells and jumps up and down, the huge collection of medals covering his uniform clash together*] Come on, Mr P, let's have some really super-duper explosions!

MISS TIBBS [*Demandingly*]: Silence, you silly boy! [*The* CHIEF OF STAFF *sits on the floor with his thumb in his mouth*]

PRESIDENT: Listen, the point is this. *Who are they?* And *where do they come from?* What do you think, Nanny?

MISS TIBBS [*Matter-of-factly*]: Well, it's hard to say, but it could be the Russians.

PRESIDENT: By gum, we'll soon fix this! [*Grabbing one of the many telephones on his desk*] Hello! Hello hello hello! Where's the operator? [*Jiggling feverishly with the receiver*] Operator, where are you?

MISS TIBBS: They won't answer you now, they're all watching television.

PRESIDENT: Well, *this* one'll answer! [*Snatching up a bright red telephone*] This is the hot line, directly linked to the Premier of Soviet Russia in Moscow. It's always open and only to be used in terrible emergencies! Yes, yes, you're right, Nanny, it's bound to be the Russians!
> [*All those the* PRESIDENT *talks to on the telephone should be spotlit in front of the stage but off to the same side as the* NARRATOR]

PREMIER YUGETOFF: Premier Yugetoff speaking. What's on your mind, Mr President?

PRESIDENT: Knock-knock.

PREMIER YUGETOFF: Who's there?

PRESIDENT: Warren.

PREMIER YUGETOFF: Warren who?

PRESIDENT: Warren Peace by Leo Tolstoy. Now see here, Yugetoff. You get those astronauts of yours off that Space Hotel of ours this instant! Otherwise I'm afraid we're going to have to show you just where you get off, Yugetoff!

PREMIER YUGETOFF: Those astronauts are not Russians, Mr President.

MISS TIBBS: He's lying.

PRESIDENT: You're lying.

PREMIER YUGETOFF: Not lying, sir. Have you looked closely at those astronauts in the glass box? I myself cannot see them too clearly on my TV screen, but one of them, the little one with the pointed beard and the top hat, has a distinctly Chinese look about him. In fact, he reminds me very much of my friend the Prime Minister of China.

PRESIDENT: Great garbage! [*Slamming down the red phone and picking up a porcelain one*] This porcelain phone is tied directly to the Head of the Chinese Republic in Peking. Hello hello hello!

ASST PREMIER CHU-ON-DAT: Wing's Fish and Vegetable Store in Shanghai. Mr Wing speaking.

PRESIDENT [*Crying out*]: NANNY! I thought this was a direct line to the Premier!

MISS TIBBS: It is, try again.

PRESIDENT [*Putting the phone down and picking it up again; yelling*]: HELLO!

ASST PREMIER CHU-ON-DAT: Mr Wong speaking.

PRESIDENT [*Screaming*]: MISTER WHO?

ASST PREMIER CHU-ON-DAT: Mr Wong, assistant station-master, Chunking, and if you asking about ten o'clock tlain, ten o'clock tlain no lunning today. Boiler burst.

> [*At this point the* PRESIDENT *throws the phone across the room at his* CHIEF FINANCIAL ADVISER. *It hits him in the stomach. Up to now the* CHIEF FINANCIAL ADVISER *has only been concerned with balancing a couple of books on his head. He now doubles over with the books falling to the floor*]

PRESIDENT [*Shouting*]: You're unbalanced! Can't you do anything right? Some Chief Adviser you are! What's the matter with this phone? Didn't you pay the bill?

CHIEF FINANCIAL ADVISER: It is very difficult to phone people in China, Mr President. [*Picking up the telephone and tightening some screws on it*] The country's so full of Wings and Wongs, every time you wing, you get the wong number.

PRESIDENT: You're not kidding.

CHIEF FINANCIAL ADVISER: The problem, Mr President, is that you have a screw loose.
  [*He now puts the phone back on the table for the* PRESIDENT *to use, picks up his books and tries to balance them again*]

PRESIDENT [*Again picking up the receiver*]: Hello?

ASST PREMIER CHU-ON-DAT: Gleetings, honourable Mr Plesident. Here is Assistant Plemier Chu-On-Dat speaking. How can I *do* for you?

PRESIDENT: Knock-knock.

ASST PREMIER CHU-ON-DAT: Who der?

PRESIDENT: Ginger.

ASST PREMIER CHU-ON-DAT: Ginger who?

PRESIDENT: Ginger yourself much when you fell off the Great Wall of China? Okay, Chu-On-Dat. Let me speak to Premier How-Yu-Bin.

ASST PREMIER CHU-ON-DAT: Much regret Premier How-Yu-Bin not here just this second, Mr Plesident.

PRESIDENT: Where is he?

ASST PREMIER CHU-ON-DAT: He outside mending a flat tyre on his 'Made-in-Hong-Kong' bicycle.

PRESIDENT: On no, he isn't. You can't fool me, you crafty old mandarin! At this very minute he's boarding our magnificent Space Hotel with seven other rascals to blow it up!

ASST PREMIER CHU-ON-DAT: Excuse please, Mr Plesident. You make big mistake.

PRESIDENT [*Barking*]: No mistake! And if you don't call them off right away I'm going to tell my military Chief of Staff to blow them all sky high! So chew on that, Chu-On-Dat!

[*Spotlight off 'foreign premier' area*]

CHIEF OF STAFF [*Shouting*]: Hooray! Let's blow every-one up! Bang-bang! Bang-bang!

MISS TIBBS [*Screaming at him*]: SILENCE!

CHIEF FINANCIAL ADVISER [*Almost in disbelief*]: I've done it! I'VE DONE IT! Look at me, everybody! I've balanced the budget!
    [*He stands proudly with books labelled 'Budget' on his head, balancing gingerly. Everyone applauds. Now spotlight on* ASTRONAUTS]

SHUCKWORTH [*Urgently interrupting*]: They've linked up and gone on board! And they've taken in the bed ... I mean the bomb! [*Silent pause*] I repeat, they've gone on board and taken the bomb with them!
    [*The* PRESIDENT *now goes over to the microphone*]

PRESIDENT [*Ordering in an authoritative voice*]: Stay well clear of them, Shuckworth! There's no point in getting your boys blown up as well.

NARRATOR [*Spotlight as* NARRATOR *stands off to the side; fade other two spots out as he/she speaks*]: And now, all over the world, the millions of watchers wait more tensely than ever in front of their television sets. The picture on their screens, in vivid colour, shows the sinister little glass box securely linked up to the underbelly of the gigantic Space Hotel. It looks like some tiny baby animal clinging to its mother. And when the camera zooms closer, it is clear for all to see that the glass box is completely empty. All eight of the desperados have climbed into the Space Hotel earlier ... and it seems as though they've taken their bomb with them. As a matter of fact, I think they should be coming into camera-view very soon ... Oh, by the way, I shouldn't expect them to come floating in, if I were you, due to the gravity-making machine, of course. They should really have come into view by now. I wonder what is keeping ... Oh, there they are! Do you see them. Yes ... yes ... they're inside the Space Hotel!

> [*Spotlight off* NARRATOR *and curtain opens showing a large room of the Space Hotel, the lobby. Aside from some incidental furniture there should be five elevator doors in view. All eight enter in awe of the beauty and splendour of the room. When one of the* GRANDPARENTS *acts like he/she is going to talk,* MR WONKA *puts his finger to his lips emphatically, goes over to a small bulletin board and writes in large bold letters,* 'DON'T SAY A WORD! SPACE CONTROL IN HOUSTON IS PROBABLY LISTENING!' *From now on*

Ground Control will only be heard over a loudspeaker, and not seen. Remember to have GRANDPARENTS *pushed on and remaining in bed*]

GROUND CONTROL [*In a booming voice*]: ATTENTION! [*Everybody jumps*] Attention the eight foreign astronauts! This is Space Control in Houston, Texas, U.S.A.! You are trespassing on American property! You are ordered to identify yourselves immediately! Speak now! [MR WONKA *again keeps everyone quiet by putting his finger to his lips, as if to indicate 'Ssshh'*] Who are you? I repeat ... Who ... are you? [*Pause*] SPEAK! SPEAK! SPEAK! SPEAK! [GRANDMA GEORGINA *shoots under the sheet.* GRANDMA JOSEPHINE *sticks her fingers in her ears.* GRANDPA GEORGE *buries his head in the pillow.* MR *and* MRS BUCKET, *both petrified, are in each other's arms.* CHARLIE *is clutching* GRANDPA JOE'S *hand, and the two of them are staring at* MR WONKA *and seemingly begging him with their eyes to do something.* MR WONKA *is standing very still and looking very calm and thoughtful*] This is your last chance! You cannot fool us! Your phoney costumes are not going to help you! We are asking you once more ... Who ...are ... you? Reply immediately! If you do not reply we shall be forced to regard you as dangerous enemies. We shall then press the emergency freezer switch and the temperature in the Space Hotel will drop to minus one hundred degrees centigrade. All of you will be instantly deep-frozen. You have fifteen seconds to speak. After that you will turn into icicles ...One ... two ... three ...

CHARLIE [*Half-whispering*]: Grandpa, we must do something. We *must*! Quick!

GROUND CONTROL: Seven ... eight ... nine ...
[MR WONKA *now springs to life. He spins round on his toes, skips a few paces across the floor and then, in a frenzied unearthly sort of scream, cries out*]

MR WONKA: FIMBO FEEZI!
[*The loudspeaker stops counting and there is a dead silence*]

MR WONKA: BUNGO BUNI! BUNGO BUNI ... DAFU DUNI ... YUBEE LUNI! [*Brief silence again*] ZOONK-ZOONK-ZOONK-ZOONK-ZOONK! [MR WONKA *now moves towards the loudspeaker (audience) and displays confidence and authority in his manner, speaking slowly but firmly*]

Kirasuku malibuku,
 Weebee wize un yubee kuku!

Alipenda kakemenda,
Pantz forldun ifno suspenda!

Funikika kanderika,
Weebee stronga yubee weeka!

Popokota borumoka
Veri riski yu provoka!

Katikati moons un stars
Fanfanisha Venus Mars!

[MR WONKA *then pauses dramatically for a few seconds. He takes an enormous deep breath and in a wild and fearsome voice, he yells out*]

KITIMBIBI ZOONK!
FIMBOLEEZI ZOONK!
GUGUMIZA ZOONK!
FUMIKAKA ZOONK!
ANAPOLALA ZOONK ZOONK
ZOONK!

[*Spotlight on Presidential Study area (formerly Ground Control). Fade stage light leaving characters in frozen-action*]

PRESIDENT [*Crying out in fright*]: NANNY! Oh, Nanny, what on earth do we do now?

MISS TIBBS [*Calmly*]: I'll get you a nice warm glass of milk.

PRESIDENT: I hate the stuff! Please don't make me drink it!

MISS TIBBS: Then summon the Chief Interpreter.

PRESIDENT: Yes, summon the Chief Interpreter! Where is he?
> [*Enter the* CHIEF INTERPRETER *for the first time*]

CHIEF INTERPRETER: Right here, Mr President.

PRESIDENT: What language was that creature spouting up there in the Space Hotel? Be quick! Was it Eskimo, Tagalog, or Ugro?

CHIEF INTERPRETER: None of those, Mr President.

PRESIDENT: Was it Tulu, then? Or Tangus, or Tupi?

CHIEF INTERPRETER: None of those either, Mr President.

MISS TIBBS [*Yelling impatiently*]: Don't just stand there telling him what it *wasn't*, you idiot! Tell him what it *was*!

CHIEF INTERPRETER: Yes, ma'am, Miss Vice-

President, ma'am. [*He is now beginning to shake with fear of Miss Tibbs*] Believe me, Mr President, it was not a language I have ever heard before.

PRESIDENT: But I thought you knew every language in the world.

CHIEF INTERPRETER: I do, Mr President.

PRESIDENT: Don't lie to me, Chief Interpreter. How can you possibly know every language in the world when you don't know this one?

CHIEF INTERPRETER: That's just it, it's not a language of this world, Mr President.

MISS TIBBS [*Barking out*]: Nonsense, man! I understand some of it myself!

CHIEF INTERPRETER: These people, Miss Vice-President, ma'am, have obviously tried to learn just a few of our easier words, but the rest of it is a language that has never been heard before on this earth!

PRESIDENT [*Crying out*]: SCREAMING SCORPIONS! You mean to tell me they could be coming from ... from ... from *somewhere else*?

CHIEF INTERPRETER: Precisely, Mr President.

PRESIDENT: Like where?

CHIEF INTERPRETER: Who knows? But did you not notice, Mr President, how they used the words Venus and Mars?

PRESIDENT: Of course I noticed it, but what's that got to do with it? ... Ah-ha! I see what you're driving at! Good gracious me! Men from Mars ... and Venus! That could make for trouble.

CHIEF INTERPRETER: I'll say it could!

MISS TIBBS: He wasn't talking to you!

PRESIDENT: What do we do now, General?

CHIEF OF STAFF [*Crying out*]: Blow 'em up!

PRESIDENT [*Crossly*]: You're always wanting to blow things up. Can't you think of something *else*?

CHIEF OF STAFF: I like blowing things up! It makes such a lovely noise. WOOMPH-WOOMPH!

MISS TIBBS: Don't be a fool! If you blow these people

up, Mars will declare war on us! So will Venus!

PRESIDENT: Quite right, Nanny, we'd be troculated like turkeys, every one of us! We'd be mashed like potatoes!

CHIEF OF STAFF [*Shouting*]: I'll take 'em on!

MISS TIBBS [*Snapping back*]: SHUT UP! YOU'RE FIRED!

EVERYONE [*Except* CHIEF OF STAFF]: Hooray! Well done, Miss Vice-President, ma'am!

MISS TIBBS: We've got to treat these fellows gently. The one who spoke just now sounded extremely cross. We've got to be polite to them, butter them up, make them happy. The last thing we want is to be invaded by men from Mars. You've got to talk to them, Mr President. Tell Ground Control in Houston we want another direct radio link with the Space Hotel! And hurry!

PRESIDENT [*Going over to microphone*]: Houston Ground Control! Houston Ground Control ... this is the President! Give me another direct radio link. With the Space Hotel this time, if you please.
    [*No spotlight on Ground Control – sound only. They*

will only be heard over the loudspeaker, as the PRESIDENT *was when he first talked to the* ASTRONAUTS]

GROUND CONTROL: Yes sir Mr President, sir ... Now hear this! Now hear this! You on the Space Hotel ... The President of the United States will now address you!

> [GRANDMA GEORGINA'S *head peeps cautiously out from under the sheets as the stage lights are once again brought up and all characters in the Space Hotel begin to move again out of frozen-action positions.* GRANDMA JOSEPHINE *takes her fingers out of her ears and* GRANDPA GEORGE *lifts his face from the pillow*]

PRESIDENT [*In a too nice voice*]: Dear, *dear* friends! Welcome to Space Hotel *U.S.A.* Greetings to the brave astronauts from Mars and Venus ...

CHARLIE [*In a half-whisper*]: Mars and Venus! You mean he thinks we're from ...

MR WONKA [*Doubling up with silent laughter, shaking all over and hopping from one foot to the other*]: Ssshh-ssshh-ssshh!

PRESIDENT: You have come a long way, so why don't

you come just a tiny bit farther and pay *us* a visit down here on our humble little Earth? I invite all eight of you to stay with me here in Washington as my honoured guests. You could land that wonderful glass space machine of yours on the lawn in back of the White House. We shall have the red carpet out and ready. I do hope you know enough of our language to understand me. I shall wait most anxiously for your reply.

> [MR WONKA, *still shaking with laughter, goes and sits down on the bed and signals everyone to gather round close*]

MR WONKA [*Half-whispering*]: They're scared to death. They won't bother us any more now. So let's have that feast we were talking about and afterwards we can explore the hotel.

GRANDMA JOSEPHINE [*Half-whispering*]: Aren't we going to the White House? I want to go to the White House and stay with the President.

MR WONKA: My dear old dotty dumpling, you look as much like a man from Mars as a bedbug! They'd know at once they'd been fooled. We'd be arrested before we could say how d'you do.

> [*Everyone seems to nod in agreement with* MR WONKA, *who now begins to write something on a piece of paper*]

CHARLIE [*Half-whispering*]: But we've got to say *some-thing* to him. He must be sitting down there in the White House this very minute waiting for an answer.

MR BUCKET: Make an excuse.

MRS BUCKET: Tell him we're otherwise engaged.

GRANDPA JOE: Ask him if we can come another time.

MR WONKA [*Half-whispering*]: You are right. It is rude to ignore an invitation.

> [*At this point* MR WONKA *stands up and walks a few paces forward from the group. He begins to speak with a voice like that of a giant, deep and mysterious and ominous. He reads what he speaks from the paper he was writing on*]

In the quelchy quaggy sogmire,
In the mashy mideous harshland,
At the witchy hour of gloomness,
All the grobes come oozing home.

You can hear them softly sliming,
Glissing hissing o'er the slubber,
All those oily boily bodies
Oozing onward in the gloam.

So start to run! Oh, skid and daddle,
Through the slubber slush and sossel!
Skip jump hop and try to skaddle!
All the grobes are on the roam!

PRESIDENT [*Crying out*]: Jumping jackrabbits! I think they're after us!

EX-CHIEF OF STAFF [*Pleading*]: Oh, *please* let me blow them up!

MISS TIBBS [*Yelling*]: *Silence!* Now, go stand in the corner!
    [*The* EX-CHIEF OF STAFF *does exactly as* MISS TIBBS *says, while putting his thumb in his mouth, hanging his head and generally looking as if he has just had a severe beating*]

GRANDMA JOSEPHINE [*Fiercely, loudly, piercingly, and in a real attention-getting manner*]: EEEEE-AAAAAAHHHHHHHHHHHHHHHHHH GGGGGGGGHHHH...IIIIIIIEEEEEEE EEEEEEAAAAAAGGGGGGGGGHHH HH!!!!!!!! [*This scream will draw everyone's attention to what* GRANDMA JOSEPHINE *is now pointing at with a shaking finger in the elevator doorway. Everyone can clearly see that there is something ... something thick ... brown ... well actually greenish-brown ... with a slimy-*

looking skin and large eyes ... squatting inside the elevator. GRANDMA JOSEPHINE *now screams again, but not nearly as long. Spotlight off* PRESIDENT] EEEAA AAGGGHHHHHIIIEEE!!!

[*At this point everyone is aghast at what they see. Everyone is frozen in fear except for* CHARLIE *and* MR WONKA, *who are also very hesitant*]

CHARLIE: Look, Mr Wonka! The other four elevator doors are opening also! Ohhh ... aren't they ugly? I wonder what or who they are? Wait! What ... what's going ... on ... Look, Mr Wonka ... they ... they ... they're starting to change shape ...

[*Immediately fade stage lights so that letter changes can be made in elevators and bring up spotlight on the* PRESIDENT. *Have him interrupting loudly to divert the attention of the audience*]

PRESIDENT [*Very loud and demanding*]: What's going on up there? Why has it been so quiet? What was that loud ferocious scream? Who screamed like that? Does anyone know what is going on? Houston! HOUSTON! Do you read me? Are you there, Houston? Come on Ground Control ... answer!

GROUND CONTROL [*Not spotlit but coming over a speaker*]: Yes sir, Mr President, sir. We read you, loud and clear.

PRESIDENT: Well then, tell me what is going on up there!

GROUND CONTROL: We don't know, sir. It's awfully weird ...

[*Brighten stage lights and dim spotlight on the* PRESIDENT *as* CHARLIE *interrupts*]

CHARLIE: Mr Wonka! What kinds of shapes have they changed into? If I didn't know any better, I'd think that they were ... no ... that's ridiculous ... but they sure look like ... no ... they couldn't be ...

MR WONKA: Yes, yes, Charlie! You're right! It may seem ridiculous ... but they've ... they've ... they've changed into *letters*!

CHARLIE: Not just letters, Mr Wonka, but letters that seem to spell something! Let's see ... S ... [*Slight pause*] ... C ... [*Slight pause*] ... R ... [*Slight pause*] ... A ... [*Slight pause*] ... M ... humph ... S-C-R-A-M ... say ... that spells ...

MR WONKA [*Interrupting loudly and anxiously*]: That spells SCRAM! That means LEAVE! It means BEAT IT! It means GET OUT QUICK! C'mon ... HURRY! [*Everyone rushes immediately and frantically off stage with* MR WONKA *leading the way*

repeating wildly] SCRAM, SCRAM, SCRAM!
[*Curtain; old ones pushed off in bed*]

End of Scene 4
Interval if desired

SCENE 5

NARRATOR *enters in front of curtain off to the side as usual: spotlight.*

NARRATOR [*Acting frightened*]: Oh, my goodness! Oh, my gracious! Oh, my golly! What a narrow escape! What a near miss! What good fortune for our friends! [*Taking a deep breath*] Whew ... Weren't those terrible things ferocious? [*Pause*] Well ... I'm glad Mr Wonka and Charlie and the rest of the crew got off the Space Hotel safely! They almost didn't! But, listen ... did you hear that? It sounds as if the Great Glass Elevator just undocked itself from the Hotel ... [*Pauses and acts as if he's listening*] Yes ... I'm sure of it ... they're away ... what a relief ... You know ... I wonder ... I wonder just what they are all thinking and saying in the Great Glass Elevator right about now. And what's more ... I wonder what those horrifying disgusting things really were! Boy, I hope that's the last we see of them. [*Pause*] Well ... I'm sure they're gone now ... everybody's safe, at last. *Say* ... would you like to look in on the Great Glass Elevator with me? [*Pause*] *Sure* ... why not? Let's go ...

[*Curtain opens: spotlight off. Use usual lighting for*

Great Glass Elevator and remember characters should again behave in a 'weightless' fashion]

MR WONKA [*Gasping*]: Oh, my goodness me! Oh, my sainted pants! Oh, my painted ants! Oh, my crawling cats! I hope never to see anything like *that* again!

CHARLIE: But who *were* those awful creatures?

MR WONKA: You mean you didn't know? Well, it's a good thing you didn't. If you'd had even the faintest idea of what horrors you were up against, you'd have been fossilized with fear and glued to the ground! Then they'd have got you! You'd have been a cooked cucumber! You'd have been rasped into a thousand tiny bits, grated like cheese and flocculated alive! They'd have made necklaces from your knucklebones and bracelets from your teeth! Because those creatures, my dear ignorant boy, are the most brutal, vindictive, venomous, murderous beasts in the entire universe! [*Louder*] VERMICIOUS KNIDS! That's what they were ... VERMICIOUS KNIDS!

CHARLIE: I thought they were grobes. Those oozy-woozy grobes you were telling the President about.

MR WONKA: Oh, no, I just made those up to scare the

White House. But there is nothing made up about Vermicious Knids, believe you me. They live, as everybody knows, on the planet Vermes, which is eighteen thousand four hundred and twenty-seven million miles away, and they are very, very clever brutes indeed. The Vermicious Knid can turn itself into any shape it wants. It has no bones. Its body is really one huge muscle, enormously strong, but very stretchy and squishy, like a mixture of rubber and putty with steel wires inside. Normally it is egg-shaped, but it can just as easily give itself two legs like a human, or four legs like a horse. It can become as round as a ball or as long as a kite-string. From fifty yards away, a fully grown Vermicious Knid could stretch out its neck and bite your head off without even getting up!

GRANDMA GEORGINA: Bite your head off with what? I didn't see any mouth.

MR WONKA [*Mysteriously*]: They have other things to bite with.

GRANDMA GEORGINA [*Demandingly*]: Such as *what*?

MR WONKA: Ring off, your time's up. But listen everybody. I've just had a funny thought. There I was kidding around with the President and pretending we were creatures from some other planet and by golly, there actually *were* creatures from some other planet on board!

CHARLIE: Do you think there were many? More than the five we saw?

MR WONKA: Thousands! There are five hundred rooms in that Space Hotel and there's probably a family of them in every room!

GRANDPA JOE: Somebody's going to get a nasty shock when they go on board!

MR WONKA: They'll be eaten like peanuts, every one of them.

CHARLIE: You don't really mean that, do you, Mr Wonka?

MR WONKA: Of course I mean it. These Vermicious Knids are the terror of the Universe. They travel through space in great swarms, landing on other stars and planets and destroying everything they find. There used to be some rather nice creatures living on the moon a long time ago. They were called Poozas. But the Vermicious Knids ate the lot. They did the same on Venus and Mars and many other planets.

CHARLIE: Then why haven't they come down to our Earth and eaten us?

MR WONKA: They've tried to, Charlie, many times, but they've never made it. You see, all around our earth there is a vast envelope of air and gas, and anything hitting *that* at high speed gets red-hot. Space capsules are made of special heat-proof metal, and when they make a re-entry, their speeds are reduced right down to about two thousand miles an hour, first by retro-rockets and then by something called 'friction'. But even so, they get badly scorched. Knids, which are not heat-proof at all, and don't have any retro-rockets, get sizzled up completely before they're halfway through. Have you ever seen a shooting star?

CHARLIE: Lots of them.

MR WONKA: Actually, they're not shooting stars at all. They're Shooting *Knids*. They're Knids trying to enter the earth's atmosphere at high speed and going up in flames.

GRANDMA GEORGINA: What rubbish!

MR WONKA: You wait. You may see it happening before the day is done.

CHARLIE: But if they're so fierce and dangerous, why didn't they eat us up right away in the Space Hotel? Why did they waste time twisting their bodies into letters and writing SCRAM?

MR WONKA: Simple, because they're show-offs! They're tremendously proud of being able to write like that.

GRANDPA JOE: If that's true, why say SCRAM when they wanted to catch us and eat us?

MR WONKA: It's the only word they know! Dreadfully boring creatures, you know. Oh, they're terrible all right, but dreadfully boring and tiresome. [*Voice trailing off*] Very ... very ... very ... boring ...
    [*Lights go dim, characters in frozen action, spotlight on* PRESIDENT'S *office again. Curtain closes slowly during next action*]

PRESIDENT [*Interrupting loudly*]: Well, what do you think men ... er ... and ... uh ... Miss Tibbs, of course, and Mrs Taubsypuss, my cat? Do you think the men from Mars have accepted my invitation to the White House?

CHIEF INTERPRETER: Of course they have. It was a brilliant speech, sir.

MISS TIBBS: They're probably on their way down here right now! Go and wash that nasty sticky chewing gum off your fingers quickly. They could be here any minute.

PRESIDENT: Let's have a song first! Please sing another one about me, Nanny?

MISS TIBBS: Well ... if everyone insists ... [*Sheepishly*] Ahem ... well ... here goes ... [*Everyone except the* PRESIDENT *winces in pain*]

> This mighty man of whom I sing,
> the greatest of them all,
> was once a teeny little thing,
> just eighteen inches tall.

> I used to wash between his toes,
> and cut his little nails.
> I brushed his hair and wiped his nose
> and weighed him on the scales.

> Through happy childhood days he strayed,
> as all nice children should.
> I smacked him when he disobeyed,
> and stopped when he was good.

> It soon began to dawn on me
> he wasn't very bright,
> because when he was twenty-three
> he couldn't read or write.

'What shall we do?' his parents sob.
'The boy has got the vapours.'
He couldn't even get a job
delivering the papers!

'Ah-ha,' I said, 'this little clot
could be a politician.'
'Nanny,' he cried, 'oh Nanny, what
a super proposition!'

'Okay,' I said, 'let's learn and note
the art of politics.
Let's teach you how to miss the boat
and how to drop some bricks,
and how to win the people's vote
and lots of other tricks.

Let's learn to make a speech a day
upon the TV screen,
in which you never say
exactly what you mean.
And most important, by the way,
is not to let your teeth decay,
and keep your fingers clean.'

And now that I am eighty-nine,
it's too late to repent.
The fault was mine the little swine
became the President.

PRESIDENT [*Happily*]: Bravo Nanny!

OTHERS [*In phony approval*]: Hooray! Well done, Miss Vice-President, ma'am! Brilliant! Tremendous!
[*Spotlight now on* ASTRONAUTS *also and* SHUCKWORTH *interrupts this shallow celebration*]

SHUCKWORTH: Mr President, sir! Mr President, sir! Request permission to link up and go aboard Space Hotel?

PRESIDENT: Permission granted! Go right ahead, Shuckworth. It's all clear now ... Thanks to me.
[*Spotlight out on* ASTRONAUTS; *all of stage area dark and clear of people as an almost ominous silence begins*]

PRESIDENT: Hey, there! We've lost our television picture, Shuckworth!
[*At this point, the audience can only hear the* ASTRONAUTS]

SHUCKWORTH: I'm afraid the camera got smashed against the side of the Space Hotel, Mr President! You won't be able to see anything, I'm afraid, but we'll keep you posted on everything that happens!
[*The* PRESIDENT *pounds his fist on the table with*

frustration and jumps up and down with a tantrum]

SHUCKWORTH [*Interrupting the antics of the* PRESI-DENT]: All astronauts and one hundred and fifty hotel staff safely aboard Space Hotel! We are now standing in the lobby!

PRESIDENT: And what do you think of it all?

SHUCKWORTH: Gee, Mr President, it's just *great*! It's *unbelievable*! It's so *enormous*! And so ... it's kind of hard to find words to describe it, it's so truly grand – especially the chandeliers and the carpets and all! I have the Chief Hotel Manager, Mr Walter W. Wall, beside me now. He would like the honour of a word with you, sir.

PRESIDENT: Put him on.

WALTER WALL: Mr President, sir, this is Walter Wall. What a sumptuous hotel this is! The decorations are superb!

PRESIDENT: Have you noticed that all the carpets are wall to wall, Mr Walter Wall?

WALTER WALL: I have indeed, Mr President.

PRESIDENT: All the wallpaper is wall to wall, too, Mr Walter Wall.

WALTER WALL: Yes, sir, Mr President! Isn't that something! It's going to be a real pleasure running a beautiful hotel like this! Hey! What's going on over there? Something's coming out of the elevators! HELP! AYEEEEE! OWWWW! YEEEE! HEL-L-LP! HEL-L-L-LP! HEL-L-L-L-L-L-P!

> [*The loudspeaker now begins to give off the most ghastly screams and yells*]

PRESIDENT: What on earth's going on? Shuckworth! Are you there, Shuckworth? ... Shanks! Showler! Mr Walter Wall! Where are you all? What's happening?

> [*The screams continue. They are so loud the* PRESIDENT *has to put his fingers in his ears. There are other noises, too — loud grunts and snortings and crunching sounds. Then silence*]

PRESIDENT: Something *nasty's* happened!

EX-CHIEF OF STAFF: It's those men from Mars! I told you to let me blow them up!

PRESIDENT: SILENCE! I've got to think!

> [*The loudspeaker begins to crackle*]

SHUCKWORTH: Hello! Hello hello! Are you receiving me, Space Control in Houston?

PRESIDENT [*Grabbing the mike on his desk*]: Leave this to me, Houston! [*Shouting*] President Gilligrass here, receiving you loud and clear! Go ahead!

SHUCKWORTH: Astronaut Shuckworth here, Mr President, back aboard the Commuter Capsule – [*With a sigh of relief*] thank *goodness*!

PRESIDENT: What happened, Shuckworth? Who's with you?

SHUCKWORTH: We're most of us here, Mr President, I'm glad to say. Shanks and Showler are with me, and a whole bunch of other folks. I guess we lost maybe a couple of dozen people altogether, pastry chefs, hall porters, that sort of thing. It was a scramble getting out of that place alive!

PRESIDENT [*Shouting*]: What do you mean you *lost two dozen people*? How did you lose them?

SHUCKWORTH: Gobbled up! One gulp and that was it! I saw a big six-foot-tall assistant manager being swallowed up just like you'd swallow a lump of ice cream, Mr President! No chewing – nothing. Just down the hatch!

PRESIDENT [*Yelling*]: But *who*? Who are you talking about? Who did the swallowing?

SHUCKWORTH [*Crying out*]: HOLD IT! Oh, my gracious, here they all come now! They're coming after us! They're swarming out of the Space Hotel! They're coming out in swarms! You'll have to excuse me a moment, Mr President. No time to talk right now ...

End of Scene 5

SCENE 6

Spotlight off and curtain opens showing Great Glass Elevator in middle of stage, as usual. Stage lights are brought up and all characters now move out of previous frozen-action positions.

CHARLIE [*Shouting*]: There's something ahead! Can you see it, Grandpa Joe? Straight in front of us!

GRANDPA JOE [*With enthusiasm*]: I can, Charlie, I can ... Good grief! It's the Space Hotel!

CHARLIE [*Amazed*]: It can't be, Grandpa. We left it miles behind us long ago.

MR WONKA: Ah-ha. We've been going so fast we've gone all the way around the earth and caught up with it again. [*Proudly*] A splendid effort, if I do say so myself ... a splendid effort!

CHARLIE: And there's the Commuter Capsule! Can you see it, Grandpa? It's just behind the Space Hotel!

GRANDPA JOE: There's something else there, too, Charlie, if I'm not mistaken!

GRANDMA JOSEPHINE [*Screaming*]: I KNOW WHAT THOSE ARE! They're Vermicious Knids! Turn back at once!

GRANDMA GEORGINA [*Yelling*]: REVERSE! [*Drawn-out cry*] Go the other way!

MR WONKA: Dear lady, this isn't an automobile on the highway. When you are in orbit, you cannot stop and you cannot go backwards. You need to stop this nonsense once and for all. There is nothing to fear, for my Elevator is completely Knid-proof . . .

CHARLIE [*Interrupting in a fearful voice*]: They're attacking it! They're after the Commuter Capsule!

GRANDPA JOE [*Describing the action*]: It's a fearsome sight. The huge green egg-shaped Knids are grouping themselves into squadrons with about twenty Knids to a squadron. Each squadron is forming itself into a line abreast, with one yard between Knids. Oh, my goodness, one after another, the squadrons are attacking the Commuter Capsule. They're attacking in reverse with their pointed bottoms in front and they're coming in at a fantastic speed! WHAM! One squadron has attacked, bounced off and wheeled away. CRASH! Another squadron has just smashed against the side of the Commuter Capsule!

CHARLIE: We must help them! [*Desperately*] We've got to do something! There are a hundred and fifty people inside that thing!

> [*Dim stage lights with Great Glass Elevator characters returning to frozen-action positions which will only be temporary. Spotlight on* PRESIDENT'S *Study.* ASTRONAUTS *are not seen, but heard over a speaker*]

SHUCKWORTH [*Shouting*]: They're ... They're ... coming at us in droves! They're bashing us to bits!

PRESIDENT [*Yelling*]: But *who?* You haven't even told us who's attacking you!

SHUCKWORTH: These dirty great greenish-brown brutes with red eyes!

SHANKS [*Butting in*]: They're shaped like enormous eggs and they're coming at us backwards.

PRESIDENT [*Surprised*]: *Backwards?* Why backwards?

SHUCKWORTH [*Shouting*]: Because their bottoms are even more pointy than their tops! Look out! Here comes another lot! [*Band noise*] We won't be able to stand this much longer, Mr President! What shall we do, Mr President, sir? What on earth shall we do?

PRESIDENT [*Shouting*]: Fire your rockets, you idiot, and make a re-entry! Come back to Earth immediately!

SHOWLER [*Shouting*]: That's impossible! They've busted our rockets! They've smashed them to smithereens!

SHANKS [*Shouting*]: We're *cooked*, Mr President! We're done for! Because even if they *don't* succeed in destroying the Capsule, we'll have to stay up here in orbit for the rest of our lives! We *can't* make a re-entry without rockets! [*Pause: the* PRESIDENT *behaves frantically because he doesn't know what to do*] Any moment now, Mr President, we're going to lose contact with you altogether! There's another lot coming at us from the left and they're aiming straight for our radio antenna. HERE THEY COME! I don't think we'll be able to ...
　　　[*Dead silence over the speaker now*]

PRESIDENT [*Crying out*]: SHANKS! Where are you, Shanks ...? Shuckworth! Shanks! Showler ...! Shucks! Shankler ...! SHANKSWORTH! SHOWL! SHUCKLER! Why don't you answer me?!
　　　[*Spotlight off* PRESIDENT'S *Study; bring up stage lights on Great Glass Elevator with characters again moving out of frozen-action positions*]

CHARLIE: Surely their only hope is to make a re-entry and dive back to earth quickly.

MR WONKA: Yes, but in order to re-enter the earth's atmosphere they've got to kick themselves out of orbit. They've got to change course and head downward and to do that they need rockets! But their rocket tubes are all dented and bent! You can see that from here! They're crippled!

CHARLIE: Why can't we tow them down?
　　[MR WONKA *jumps up and down*]

MR WONKA [*Jumping up and down and crying out enthusiastically*]: Charlie! You've got it! That's it! We'll tow them out of orbit! To the buttons, quick!

GRANDPA GEORGE: What do we tow them with? [*Sarcastically*] Our neckties?

MR WONKA: Don't you worry about a little thing like that! [*Confidently*] My Great Glass Elevator is ready for anything! In we go!

GRANDMA JOSEPHINE [*Screaming*]: STOP HIM!

GRANDPA JOE: You be quiet, Josie! There's someone over there needs a helping hand and it's our job to give it! If you're frightened, you'd better just close your eyes tight and stick your fingers in your ears!

[*That's exactly what she does*]

MR WONKA [*Shouting*]: Grandpa Joe, sir! Kindly jet yourself over to the far corner of the Elevator there and turn that handle! It lowers the rope!

GRANDPA JOE: A rope's no good, Mr Wonka! The Knids will bite through a rope in one second!

MR WONKA: It's a steel rope! It's made of reinscorched steel. If they try to bite through *that*, their teeth will splinter like spillikins! To your buttons, Charlie! You've got to help me manoeuvre. We're going right over the top of the Commuter Capsule and then we'll try to hook on to it somewhere and get a firm hold!

[NARRATOR *enters in front of curtain off to the side as usual; spotlight on* NARRATOR *as activity continues on Great Glass Elevator. Elevator rocks back and forth from being hit by Knids: this diversion will allow steel rope to be extended*]

NARRATOR [*Excitedly*]: Oh, boy ... what action! Just look at that Great Glass Elevator! Just look at our heroes! Why, the Elevator is just like a battleship going into action! It's a good thing it's Knid-proof! Now that the Elevator has moved smoothly over the enormous Commuter Capsule, the Knids have stopped attacking the Capsule and have gone for the Great Glass Elevator. Just look at the beating it's taking from squadron after squadron of giant Vermicious Knids flinging themselves against Mr Wonka's marvellously magnificent, mysterious machine! [*Crashing noises over speaker*] What a noise! It's terrible! Oh dear, the Elevator is being tossed about the sky like a leaf ... and inside ... inside is ... well ... Grandma Josephine, Grandma Georgina and Grandpa George are just floating around and yowling and screeching and flapping their arms and calling for help. [*Pause so yowling and screeching can take place for a few moments and then tail off*] And just look at poor Mr Bucket! His wife is wrapping her arms around him so tightly that his shirt buttons are puncturing his skin! Ahhhhh ... but just look there at Charlie and Mr Wonka ... cool as two canta-loupes working the booster-rocket controls ... and, of course, Grandpa Joe, turning the handle that unwinds the steel rope for all he is worth ... and throwing a few choice words at the Knids at the same time, I might add! Well ... no point in me going on and on! Let's go back to the Great Glass Elevator and find out what's happening!

[*Spotlight off* NARRATOR]

GRANDPA JOE [*Shouting*]: Starboard a bit, Charlie . . .
that's it . . . I think I've got it! Yes, the hook is
hooked around that stumpy thing sticking out in
front there . . . now, let's see if it will hold . . . forward
a bit . . . More! MORE! Great wonder of wonders!
Full speed ahead! She's holding fine!

MR WONKA [*Crying out*]: All boosters firing! [*He jets
himself over to* GRANDPA JOE *and shakes him exuber-
antly by the hand*] Well done, sir! You did a brilliant
job under heavy fire!

CHARLIE: Grandpa, where are the Knids? They've
suddenly vanished!
    [*Everyone is looking around*]

GRANDMA JOSEPHINE [*Crying out*]: Just a minute!
What's *that* I see over there?

CHARLIE: I hate to admit it, Grandma, but it's a
massive cloud of Vermicious Knids wheeling and
circling like a fleet of bombers!

GRANDMA GEORGINA [*Shouting*]: If you think we're
out of the woods yet, Wonka, you're crazy!

MR WONKA: I fear no Knids! We've got them beaten
now!

GRANDMA JOSEPHINE [*Yelling*]: Poppyrot and pig-wash! Any moment now they'll be at us again! Look at them! They're coming in! They're coming closer!

MRS BUCKET [*Fearfully*]: *Look!* Over there! There's one all alone! It's changing shape! It's getting longer and longer! It's slowly stretching itself out like chewing gum, becoming longer and longer and thinner and thinner! Why . . . I believe it's as long as a football field! It looks like a giant rope . . . and . . . and . . . oh my, oh dear . . . it's . . . it's . . . it's wrapping itself around us! IT'S WRAPPING ITSELF AROUND US! What shall we do?

GRANDMA JOSEPHINE [*Yelling*]: It's tying us up like a parcel!

MR WONKA: Bunkum!

GRANDMA GEORGINA [*Wailing*]: It's going to crush us in its coils!

MR WONKA: Never!
　　　　[*All this time, whenever* CHARLIE *glances back at the three* ASTRONAUTS, *he gives them the 'thumbs up' sign, but they only stare in utter disbelief*]

CHARLIE [*Crying out*]: Mr Wonka! Look at the others! What *are* they doing?

MR BUCKET [*Excited and fearful*]: I'll tell you what they're doing! They've all changed shape and become longer! Each of them has turned itself into a kind of thick rod with a curl at both ends, so that it makes a ... sort of ... double-ended hook! And now ... all the hooks are linking up into one long chain – one thousand Knids, all joining together and curving around in the sky to make a chain of Knids half a mile long or more!

MRS BUCKET [*Fearfully*]: And the one who is trying to wrap himself around us is also curling up into a hook on one end!

GRANDPA JOE [*Shouting*]: Hey! They're going to hook up with this brute who's tied himself around us!

CHARLIE [*Crying out*]: And tow us away!

GRANDMA JOSEPHINE [*Gasping*]: To the planet Vermes! Eighteen thousand four hundred and twenty-seven million miles from here!

MR WONKA [*Crying out*]: They can't do that! *We're* doing the towing around here!

CHARLIE: They're going to link up, Mr Wonka! They really are! Can't we stop them? They're going to tow us away and they're going to tow the people we're towing away as well!

GRANDMA GEORGINA [*Shrieking*]: DO SOME-THING, YOU OLD FOOL! DON'T JUST FLOAT ABOUT LOOKING AT THEM!

MR WONKA [*Embarrassed*]: I must admit that for the first time in my life I find myself at a bit of a loss.
[*They all stare in horror through the glass, in utter hopelessness*]

GRANDMA JOSEPHINE [*In a drawn-out wail*]: I want to go H ... O ... M ... E!

MR WONKA [*Crying out excitedly*]: GREAT THUN-DERING TOMCATS! *Home* is right! What on earth am I thinking of? Come on, Charlie! Quick! Re-entry! *Re-entry!* You take the yellow button! Press it for all you're worth! I'll handle this lot! [*Charlie flies over to the button*] Hold your hats! Grab your gizzards! We're going down! [*Pause*] RETRO-ROCKETS! I mustn't forget to fire the retro-rockets!

CHARLIE [*Fearfully*]: Look, Mr Wonka! The leading Knid in the chain is actually reaching out and grasping for the hook made by the Knid on the Elevator.

GRANDMA GEORGINA [*Screaming*]: We're too late! They're going to link up and haul us back!

MR WONKA [*Matter-of-factly*]: I think not. Don't you remember what happens when a Knid enters the Earth's atmosphere at high speed? He gets *red-hot*! He burns away in a long fiery trail. He becomes a Shooting Knid. Soon these dirty beasts will start popping like popcorn!
  [*A sizzling noise comes over the loudspeaker – should sound like bacon frying*]

CHARLIE [*Crying out with joy*]: They're Shooting Knids!

MR WONKA: What a splendid sight! It's better than fireworks! We've done it! [*Crying out*] They've been roasted to a crisp! They've been frizzled to a fritter! We're saved!

GRANDMA JOSEPHINE: What do you mean 'saved'? We'll all be frizzled ourselves if this goes on any longer! We'll be barbecued like beefsteaks! Look at that glass! It's hotter than a fizzgig!

MR WONKA: Have no fears, dear lady, my Elevator is air-conditioned, ventilated, aerated and automated in every possible way. We're going to be all right now.

CHARLIE: Aren't you enjoying it, Mother?

MRS BUCKET: No, I'm not. Nor is your father!

MR WONKA: Just look at the Earth down there, Charlie, getting bigger and bigger! What a great sight it is!

GRANDPA GEORGE [*Groaning*]: And us going to meet it at two thousand miles an hour! How are you going to slow down for goodness sakes? Parachutes?

MR WONKA [*With contempt*]: *Parachutes!* Parachutes are only for astronauts and sissies! And anyway, we don't want to *slow down*. We want to *speed up*! I've told you already we've got to be going at an absolutely tremendous speed when we hit. Otherwise we'll never punch our way in through the roof of the Chocolate Factory!

CHARLIE [*Anxiously*]: How about the Commuter Capsule?

MR WONKA: We'll be letting them go in a few seconds now. They *do* have parachutes, three of them, to slow them down on the last bit. Grandpa Joe, sir! Throw out the rope! Let it go! They'll be all right now so long as their parachutes are working.

GRANDPA JOE [*Calling out*]: Rope gone!
> [*Again* CHARLIE *waves at the* ASTRONAUTS *and again they do not wave back but just continue to look amazed. Spotlight off* ASTRONAUTS]

MR WONKA: It won't be long now! We shall soon know whether we are alive or dead. Keep very quiet please for this final part. I have to concentrate awfully hard, otherwise we'll come down in the wrong place. [*Pause; then, shouting*] THERE IT IS! My Chocolate Factory! My beloved Chocolate Factory!

GRANDPA JOE: You mean *Charlie's* Chocolate Factory!

MR WONKA: That's right! I'd clean forgotten I'd given it to you! I do apologize to you, my dear boy! Of course it's yours! And here we go ... Hold your breath! Hold your nose! Fasten your seat belts and say your prayers! We're going through the roof!

> [*Noise over the loudspeaker of splintering wood and lots of broken glass and crunching sounds and smashing things after curtain closes*]

End of Scene 6

SCENE 7

Characters now speak over loudspeaker unseen by audience.

MR WONKA [*Yelling*]: We're through! We've done it! We're in!

MRS BUCKET: Charlie, where in the world are we now?

CHARLIE [*Excitedly*]: We're back, Mother! We're in the Chocolate Factory!

MRS BUCKET: I'm very glad to hear it, but didn't we come rather a long way round?

MR WONKA: We had to ... to avoid the traffic.

GRANDMA GEORGINA [*Crying out*]: The man's crazy! He's round the twist! He's bogged as a beetle! He's dotty as a dingbat! He's got rats in the roof! I WANT TO GO HOME!

MR WONKA: Too late, we're there!
   [*The curtain now opens with the Great Glass Elevator*

in the same place but with Chocolate Factory scenery emphasizing chocolate. This is basically left to creative expression, but you may wish to include a chocolate river or waterfall, or trees or bushes, etc.]

GRANDMA JOSEPHINE [*Pointing offstage*]: Who in the world are all those peculiar little men?

CHARLIE: They're Oompa-Loompas! They're wonderful. You'll love them.

GRANDPA JOE: Ssshh! Listen, Charlie. The drums are starting up. They're going to sing.
[*Sound of drums offstage and choral speaking or singing also from backstage, from the supposed* OOMPA-LOOMPAS]

OOMPA-LOOMPAS:

Alleluia!
Oh alleluia and hooray!
Our Willy Wonka's back today!
We thought you'd never make it home!
We thought you'd left us all alone!
We knew that you would have to face
Some frightful creatures up in space.
We even thought we heard the crunch
Of someone eating you for lunch . . .

MR WONKA [*Shouting and laughing, raising both hands*]: All right! Thank you for your welcome!

CHARLIE: Gee, Mr Wonka ... It's *so* great to be back in your Chocolate Factory!

MR WONKA: Oh ... oh ... oh ... remember, my boy, it is now *your* Chocolate Factory! [*Thoughtfully*] But, yes, Charlie ... I know what you mean ... and there's so much more to share with you ... [*Excitedly*] with *all* of you! There is so much to share with all of you! [*He dreamily goes on as he walks forward towards the audience*] Let's see now ... there's my new recipe for making Wonka-Vite ....

CHARLIE [*Interrupting*]: Wonka-Vite? I never heard of that before, Mr Wonka!

MR WONKA [*Laughing*]: Ho ho! There are many things you have never heard of before. Yes, yes ... my Wonka-Vite ... very special ingredients in that ... yes indeedy ... very special ingredients! Hoof of a manticore, front tail of a cockatrice, the hip (and the po and the pot) of a hippopotamus, the hide (and the seek) of a spotted whangdoodle, and so on and so on ... I won't bore you with any more details ... you'll find out sooner or later, some of you anyway. Still, it really is quite a shame ...

GRANDPA JOE [*Interrupting*]: What's a shame, Mr Wonka?

MR WONKA: Oh, just the very large problem I have with Minusland and the potential of being subtracted, not to mention the Gnoolies! Yes ... yes, Wonka-Vite *does* have its problems, but then ... that's why I invented Vita-Wonk!

GRANDMA GEORGINA [*Demandingly*]: Wonka-Vite, Minusland, being subtracted, Gnoolies, Vita-Wonk ... Come on, Wonka, what is all this rubbish, anyway?

MR WONKA [*Knowingly nodding his head*]: All in good time, my dear lady. You *will*, I'm sure, find out about it, all in good time. [*Becoming much more enthusiastic*] But enough of this kind of talk! Let us now deal with the problem at hand!

GRANDPA GEORGE: What problem?

MR WONKA [*Addressing* GRANDPA GEORGE, GRANDMA GEORGINA *and* GRANDMA JOSEPHINE]: I am sure the three of you, after all this, will now want to jump out of bed and lend a hand in running the Chocolate Factory.

GRANDMA JOSEPHINE: Are you crazy? We're staying right here where we are in this nice comfortable bed, thank you very much!

> [*Large commotion offstage and one single* OOMPA-LOOMPA *enters, dressed as creatively and wildly as you can imagine him. He runs in waving his arms and carrying a huge envelope. He comes up close to* MR WONKA *and starts whispering. The three* GRANDPARENTS *and* MR *and* MRS BUCKET *shrink backwards out of fear of him*]

MR WONKA [*Loudly repeating what is being whispered to him by the* OOMPA-LOOMPA]: Outside the factory gates? Men? ... What sort of men? ... Yes, but do they look dangerous? ... Are they acting dangerously? ... And a what? ... A helicopter! ... And these men came out of it? ... They gave you this? [*He grabs the huge envelope, quickly tears it open and pulls out the folded letter inside. The* OOMPA-LOOMPA *scurries off the stage and everyone goes into frozen-action except* MR WONKA. *To ensure that all attention is on him he even does a few exciting leaps into the air before he reads the letter*] GREAT WHISTLING WHANG-DOODLES! [*Leaping so high into the air that when he lands his legs give way and he crashes onto his backside*] SNORTING SNOZZWANGERS! [*Picking himself up and waving the letter about as though he were swatting mosquitos*] Listen to this, all of you. JUST LISTEN TO THIS! [*He begins to read aloud*]

To Mr Willy Wonka

Sir

Today the entire Nation, indeed the whole world, is rejoicing at the safe return of our Commuter Capsule from space with 136 souls on board. Had it not been for the help they received from an unknown spaceship, these 136 people would never have come back. It has been reported to me that the courage shown by the eight astronauts aboard this unknown spaceship was extraordinary. Our radar stations, by tracking this spaceship on its return to Earth, have discovered that it splashed down in a place known as Wonka's Chocolate Factory. That, sir, is why this letter is being delivered to you.

I wish now to show the gratitude of the Nation by inviting all eight of those incredibly brave astronauts to come and stay in the White House for a few days as my honoured guests. I am arranging a special celebration party in the Blue Room this evening at which I myself will pin medals for bravery upon all eight of these gallant fliers. The most important persons in the land will be present at this gathering to salute the heroes whose dazzling deeds will be written forever in the

history of our Nation. Among those attending will
be the Vice-President, Miss Elvira Tibbs, all the
members of my Cabinet, my Ex-Chief of Staff and
my other military chiefs, all members of the Con-
gress ... and who else is coming? ... Oh yes, my
chief interpreter, and the Governors of every state
in the Union, and of course my cat, Mrs Taubsypuss. A helicopter awaits all eight of you outside
the factory gates. I myself await your arrival at
the White House with the very greatest pleasure
and impatience.

> I beg to remain, sir,
> Most sincerely yours,
>   Lancelot R. Gilligrass
>   President of the United States

P.S. Could you please bring me a few Wonka
Fudgemallow Delights. I love them so much but
everybody around here keeps stealing mine out of
the drawer in my desk. And don't tell Nanny.

[*While the others are still in frozen-action,* MR WONKA
*looks matter-of-factly at the letter and envelope and mutters
clearly but quietly*] Yep, this is the real thing all right,
it's even got a picture of the Presidential Seal on it
... good-looking seal too ... I saw him once in a zoo
in Kalamazoo ...

GRANDPA JOE [*Interrupting*]: YIPPPEEEEEEE!
[GRANDPA JOE *runs across the room and catches*
CHARLIE *by the hands and the two of them start dancing
away along the bank of the Chocolate River*] We're going,
Charlie! We're going to the White House!

> [MR *and* MRS BUCKET *are also dancing and laugh-
> ing and singing.* MR WONKA *seems unruffled but
> pleased as punch. After about fifteen seconds of this,
> he claps his hands for attention*]

MR WONKA [*Calling out*]: Come along, come along! We
mustn't dilly! We mustn't dally! Come on, Charlie!
And you, sir, Grandpa Joe! And Mr and Mrs
Bucket! The helicopter is outside the gates! We can't
keep it waiting!

> [*He begins hustling the four of them towards the door
> – or offstage*]

GRANDMA GEORGINA [*Screaming from the bed*]: Hey!
What about us? We were invited too, don't you
forget that!

GRANDMA JOSEPHINE [*Whining*]: It said *all eight of us*
were invited!

GRANDPA GEORGE [*Demandingly*]: And that includes
me!

MR WONKA [*Turning and looking at them*]: Of *course* it

includes you, but we can't *possibly* get that bed into a *helicopter*. It simply won't go through the door.

GRANDMA GEORGINA: You mean ... you mean if we don't get out of bed we can't come?

MR WONKA: That's *exactly* what I mean! [*Whispering an aside to* CHARLIE] Keep going, Charlie. [*Giving* CHARLIE *a little nudge*] Keep walking towards the door.
> [*Suddenly, with a large swoosh of blankets and sheets, the three old people all explode noisily out of bed at the same time and run over to* MR WONKA *and the others.* GRANDMA JOSEPHINE *suddenly stops abruptly and screams*]

GRANDMA JOSEPHINE [*Screaming*]: *Wait!* We must be mad! We can't go to a famous party in the White House in our nightshirts! We can't stand there practically naked in front of all those people while the President pins medals all over us!

GRANDMA GEORGINA [*Wailing*]: We can't go! We'll have to stay behind!

GRANDPA GEORGE: Couldn't we buy something from a store?

GRANDMA JOSEPHINE: What with? We don't have any money!

MR WONKA [*Crying out*]: *Money!* Good gracious me, don't you go worrying about money! I've got plenty of *that*!

CHARLIE: Listen! Why couldn't we ask the helicopter to land on the roof of a big department store on the way over. Then you can all pop downstairs and buy exactly what you want!

MR WONKA [*Excitedly*]: Charlie! What *would* we do without you? You're brilliant! Come along everybody! We're off to stay in the White House!
> [*They all link arms and go dancing around the Chocolate Room, down the stage stairs, and pass through the midst of the audience (with spotlights picking them up) and chanting together*]

EVERYBODY: We're off to the White House! We're off to the White House! We're off to the White House!
> [*When they have reached the middle of the audience area, CHARLIE and GRANDPA JOE make a quick and clear exchange before all eight leave the auditorium*]

GRANDPA JOE: Well, Charlie ... It's certainly been a busy day!

CHARLIE [*Laughingly*]: It's not over yet, Grandpa Joe!
It hasn't even begun!

> *Hardly a 'curtain' but certainly*
> *The End*

SOME SUGGESTIONS FOR STAGING

1. Whenever the Narrator speaks, frozen-action positions can be effectively used.

2. All houselights in the auditorium should be out for the duration of the play.

3. The Narrator can be dressed creatively for this play. A space-suit or even the appearance of an 'observer' from another world could be the costuming focus. The Narrator should have a separate spotlight at all times. A filmstrip projector is acceptable.

4. The 'foreign premier' staging area could be used exclusively for Ground Control, which would free Area 4 (see next page) for Presidential Study use only. The 'foreign premier' phone conversations would then only be heard over the sound system. This would provide more balance in the use of each staging area.

5. The loudspeaker should be a sound system in the auditorium with a microphone stand and microphone backstage on the Narrator's side. During 'loudspeaker' sequences all lines can be read back-

stage (reducing the need for memorization) and during narrations the microphone should be disengaged from the stand so that the Narrator has the freedom to move about without restriction and perform like an M.C., thus utilizing his/her personality to the full.

Staging Concept

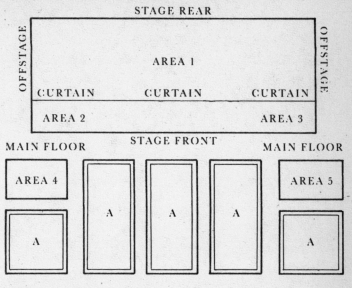

KEY

Area 1   Glass Elevator, Hotel lobby or Chocolate Room
Area 2   Astronauts and Commuter Capsule Front
Area 3   Narrator
Area 4   Ground Control or President's Study
Area 5   Foreign premiers
A   Audience

The use of spotlights, strobe lights, stage lights and a sound system will enable the audience to become a part of the production, as this approach makes the whole auditorium a stage and eliminates many cumbersome scene changes, creating a fast-moving experience in sight and sound.

SCENERY AND PROPERTIES

Great Glass Elevator

In order to fit everyone inside, you should probably use two large refrigerator boxes. Cut out one whole side of each box.

Cut a doorway out of a second side of each box.

Put totally open sides together with both doorways facing out. Connect the two boxes with strong cardboard or wood pieces to make the Elevator big enough for a bed. Attach these to large boxes with wire or nails.

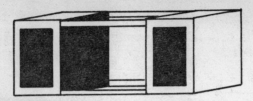

Paint and add glitter, coloured transparent paper, handle for steel rope, buttons, etc. The Elevator can be moved about on stage if it is put on a moving platform or pushed. It can also be effective just to have someone behind it, shaking it gently. Lights (particularly strobe-type) flashing at this time will also give added effect.

Grandparents' Bed
Take four chairs and place them facing each other, two by two. Separate the pairs by a couple of metres.

Lay a board across the seats of all four chairs, and cover the whole thing with a sheet or blankets.

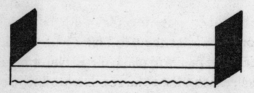

All four grandparents will now be able to sit up in the crowded bed, facing each other. If one leg of the bed is to be lifted up to show weightlessness, the chairs will have to be fastened together securely.

Solar System Stars
Cut out many cardboard squares, ranging in size from 60 centimetres by 60 centimetres to 15 centimetres by 15 centimetres. Paint stars in the squares and cut them out.

These stars can now be used in outer-space scenes, either behind the Commuter Capsule cockpit or behind the Great Glass Elevator. They can easily be hung on curtains or taped on to other objects.

Commuter Capsule Astronaut Cockpit
Cut out a large cardboard rectangle, measuring at least 1·25 metres by 2 metres. Divide the cardboard

into equal thirds, lengthwise, so that it will stand by itself and also allow room for three astronauts to sit.

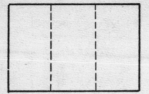

Round the two top corners and cut out the windows as shown below. Paint steel-grey and paint on any desired markings.

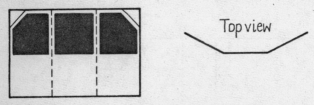

The middle portion should be forward of the two side portions, which should be bent back.

Television Screen
Cut out a piece of cardboard approximately 1·25 metres square.

Cut out the middle as shown below, leaving an uncut area at least 1 foot deep at the bottom.

Paint the screen with a control panel at the bottom. Mount it on a music stand so that the control panel covers the back of the stand. Attach with wire.

The screen can be used in the Presidential Study or Ground Control. If the Study and Ground Control are going to be in two different places, you may want to make a second screen.

Vermicious Knids
Cut out 5 cardboard rectangles, each measuring 1·25 metres by 2 metres.

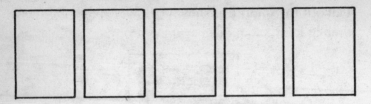

In the middle of each piece of cardboard, paint a picture of a Vermicious Knid. Paint the rest of the piece to look like an elevator.

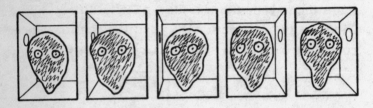

On the reverse sides of the pieces of cardboard, paint the letters S, C, R, A, M, each with a big eye in the letter (see below). Put one letter on each piece of cardboard. Paint the rest of each piece to look identical to the other side.

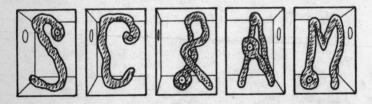

These 5 pieces of cardboard can easily be reversed in the time allowed, while distractions make the audience focus elsewhere. The Knids will then appear to have changed shape.

Chocolate River
Take a couple of large cardboard boxes and cut a wavy line through the middle of each box on all four sides.

Separate the box into two parts by cutting on the wavy line with a sharp knife. Cut off end-flaps.

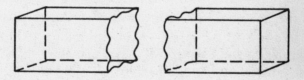

You now have two separate parts. Cut a straight line down one corner of each half.

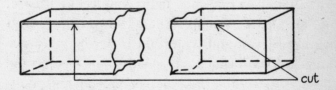

Unfold each half into a long strip.

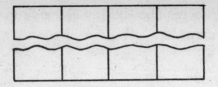

Lay the pieces next to one another, overlapping one on top of the other. Attach with staples and glue. Paint brown.

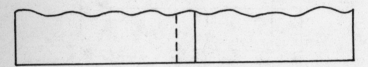

The Chocolate River can be held at both ends and moved back and forth across the stage.

Oompa-Loompas

Idea 1: On a flat piece of cardboard, sketch your own conception of an Oompa-Loompa. Cut it out and use it as a pattern to make others (if you wish to use more than one in the Chocolate Room), and paint them all.

Idea 2: Draw or trace any figure you feel best represents an Oompa-Loompa. Put your picture on an opaque projector and project the image on to a piece of stiff cardboard which is taped to a wall. Go over the projected lines with a dark marker. Cut out and paint. If the projected image is not as large as you would like, project the original picture on to a sheet of paper (just small enough to fit in the opaque projector when completed) to make it somewhat bigger. Now take the marker, outline the image and use this picture to project on to cardboard.

Idea 3: Use real children. This would be good if you have a large group and would like to get more people involved.

LIGHTING PROCEDURES

These procedures are practical if footlights, upper stage lights, a strobe light and a spotlight or two (or three) are available. If you lack any of these lights, these suggestions will still help you get a general 'feel' for the desired effects. Remember that, while your equipment may not be perfect, by using your imagination you can still provide atmosphere.

SCENE 1   *No Lights* – at beginning of play
Spotlight – on Narrator whenever he or she speaks
Spotlight 2 – on Great Glass Elevator when curtain opens
Spotlight 1 – off Narrator as he exits and all on Great Glass Elevator come to life
Footlights – red and white
Stage Uppers – red, white and blue
Footlights and Stage Uppers – fade in and out after Mr Wonka pushes brown button and Elevator shakes
Spotlight 1 – on Narrator as he briefly interrupts. Off as Charlie cuts back in. On again when Mr Wonka says to stop talking

because he wants to concentrate. Off again when Grandma Josephine screams.

LIGHTING CHANGE

All Lights – off after Mr Wonka says: 'Quick! Quick! Quick!'

Strobe – on

Footlights – blue

Stage Uppers – blue

LIGHTING CHANGE

Footlights – add red when Mr Wonka pushes 'oxygen' button

SCENE 2   *Spotlight 1* – on Narrator

All other lights – off

Spotlight 1 – off when Narrator exits

Spotlight 2 – on three astronauts

Spotlight 3 – on Ground Control as they say: 'Describe it at once!' Off after Ground Control says: 'This is desperate! This is . . .'

LIGHTING CHANGE

Spotlight 2 – off when Showler says, 'Here goes!'

Spotlight 2 – on Narrator

Footlights – red and blue, very dim and brought up slowly

Stage Uppers – red and blue, very dim and brought up slowly

LIGHTING CHANGE

Spotlight 1 – off Narrator after he says: 'What are they going to do?'

Spotlight 2 – on astronauts. Off after Showler says: 'This is scary!'

Footlights and Stage Uppers – both fully red and fully blue

SCENE 3   *Spotlight 3* – on Great Glass Elevator

Footlights and Stage Uppers – both fully red and fully blue

Strobe – on

LIGHTING CHANGE

Spotlight 2 – on astronauts

Spotlight 3 – off

Footlights and Stage Uppers – dimmed

LIGHTING CHANGE

Spotlight 2 – off after President yells: 'SILENCE! You're muddling me up.'

Spotlight 3 – on Great Glass Elevator again

Footlights and Stage Uppers – both fully red and fully blue again

SCENE 4   *All lights* – off

Spotlight 1 – on Narrator. Off Narrator when we see President for the first time

Spotlight 3 – on President

Spotlight 2 – on Premier Yugetoff. Off after he says: 'In fact, he reminds me very much

of my friend the Prime Minister of China.'
On again after President says: 'Hello hello hello!' Off again after President says: 'So chew on that, Chu-On-Dat!'

LIGHTING CHANGE

Spotlight 2 – on astronauts after Chief Financial Adviser says: 'I've balanced the budget!' Off after President says: 'There's no point in getting your boys blown up as well.'

Spotlight 3 – off at the same time as Spotlight 2

Spotlight 1 – on Narrator. Off Narrator as curtain opens to the lobby of the Space Hotel

Footlights – red, white and blue

Stage Uppers – red, white and blue

LIGHTING CHANGE

Footlights and Stage Uppers – all lights dimmed after Mr Wonka says: 'ANAPOLALA ZOONK ZOONK ZOONK!'

Spotlight 3 – on President

Footlights and Stage Uppers – all red, white and blue, fully on again after Ground Control says: 'The President of the United States will now address you!' Dim all these lights when Mr Wonka says: 'All the grobes are on the roam!' Bring lights fully up again when Miss Tibbs yells: '*Silence!* Now, go stand in the corner!'

Spotlight 3 – out on President after Grandma Josephine screams. On again after Charlie says: 'They're starting to change shape ...'

Footlights and Stage Uppers – dim all lights when the President says: 'What's going on up there?' Bring lights fully up again when Ground Control says: 'It's awfully weird ...'

Spotlight 3 – off the President

SCENE 5   *All lights* – off

Spotlight 1 – on Narrator. Off after he says: 'Let's go ...' and curtain opens.

Strobe – on

Footlights – red and blue on

Stage Uppers – red and blue on

All lights – dim and finally off as curtain closes while Mr Wonka says: 'Oh, they're terrible all right, but dreadfully boring and tiresome, very ... very ... very ... boring ...'

Spotlight 3 – on President

Spotlight 2 – on astronauts after others say: 'Tremendous!' to Miss Tibbs's song. Out

after President says: 'It's all clear now ...
Thanks to me.'

SCENE 6   *Spotlight 3* – off
Strobe – on
Footlights – red and blue on after first dim
Stage Uppers – red and blue on after first dim
All lights – dim
Spotlight 3 – on President after Charlie says:
'There are a hundred and fifty people
inside that thing!'
LIGHTING CHANGE
All lights – bring back up to red and blue
fullness
Spotlight 3 – off on President after he says:
'Why don't you answer me?'
Spotlight 1 – on Narrator after Mr Wonka
says: '... we'll try to hook on to it some-
where and get a firm hold!' Off as Grandpa
Joe says: 'Starboard a bit, Charlie ...'
Spotlight 2 – on the astronauts very briefly
after Mr Wonka responds: 'Never!' to
Grandma Georgina. This should only last
for a few seconds. Off almost immediately
Stage Uppers and House Lights – flashed on
and off repeatedly but briefly as the
Vermicious Knids become Shooting Knids
Spotlight 2 – on the astronauts very briefly

again after Grandpa Joe calls out: 'Rope gone!' This should only last for a few seconds. Off almost immediately

All lights – off after Mr Wonka says: 'We're going through the roof!'

SCENE 7   *All lights* – off until curtain opens

Spotlight 2 – on Great Glass Elevator as curtain opens

Footlights – red and white on and brought up slowly to full capacity

Stage Uppers – red and white on and brought up slowly to full capacity

All lights except for Spotlight 2 – dim as Mr Wonka reads

Spotlight 2 – on Mr Wonka as he steps forward to read the letter from the President

All lights – brought back up abruptly as Grandpa Joe yells: 'Yipppeeeeeeee!'

Spotlight 1, Spotlight 2, and Spotlight 3 all move quickly back and forth across the audience as all eight pass joyously through the midst of the audience, converging on Charlie and Grandpa Joe as they speak at the end.

Spots now dance across the room again as all exit